The Picador Book of

Birth Poems

KATE CLANCHY was born and grew up in Scotland but now lives in England. She is a popular poet: her collections *Slattern*, *Samarkand* and *Newborn* have brought her many literary awards and an unusually wide audience. She has also written extensively for Radio 4 and reviews and writes comment for the *Guardian*. She is the author of *Antigona and Me*, published by Picador. In 2009 she won the National Short Story Award.

The Picador Book of

Birth Poems

EDITED BY

Kate Clanchy

PICADOR

First published 2012 by Picador
an imprint of Pan Macmillan, a division of Macmillan Publishers Limited
Pan Macmillan, 20 New Wharf Road, London N1 9RR
Basingstoke and Oxford
Associated companies throughout the world
www.panmacmillan.com

ISBN 978-0-330-45685-2

A CIP catalogue record for this book is available from
the British Library.

Printed and bound by CPI Group (UK) Ltd, Croydon, CR0 4YY

Visit **www.picador.com** to read more about all our books
and to buy them. You will also find features, author interviews and
news of any author events, and you can sign up for e-newsletters
so that you're always first to hear about our new releases.

For my son's grandmothers,

Margaret Reynolds and Joan Clanchy,

gratefully

Contents

This New Heart
Pregnancy

To Enter That Rhythm Where the Self Is Lost
Birth

Well Done, My Lord
Thanksgiving

Hello
The First Weeks

Infant Sorrow, Infant Joy
The First Months

I Have Wished You Something
Namings and Blessings

The Thread
The First Years

Acknowledgements

Simon Armitage, 'The Keep', from *The Universal Home Doctor* by Simon Armitage, published by Faber and Faber Ltd; W. H. Auden, 'This lunar beauty', copyright © 1976, 1991, The Estate of W. H. Auden; John Berryman, 'Hello', from *Collected Poems 1937–1971* by John Berryman, published by Faber and Faber Ltd; Sujata Bhatt, '29 April 1989', from *Selected Poems*, 1977, published by Carcanet Press Limited; Kate Clanchy, 'Infant', by permission of the author; Frances Cornford, 'Mother to Child Asleep', 'The New-Born Baby's Song', 'Ode on the Whole Duty of Parents', 'On Children', by permission of Enitharmon Press; Jeni Couzyn, 'Heartsong' and 'Dawn' from *A Time to Be Born: Poems of Childbirth* (1999); Greg Delanty, 'A Circus', from *The Ship of Birth*, 2003, published by Carcanet Press Limited; Kamala Das, 'The Looking Glass', by permission of the author; Michael Donaghy, 'Haunts', by permission of the author; Carol Ann Duffy, 'Demeter', by permission of the author; Sasha Dugdale, 'Juice', 'The Funniest Bit' and 'High Office', by permission of the author; Helen Dunmore, 'The Conception', 'Scan at 8 Weeks', 'Patrick I', from *Out of the Blue: Poems 1975–2001* (Bloodaxe Books, 2001); Amir Gilboa, 'Birth' trans. Shirley Kaufman, by permission of the author; Thom Gunn, 'Baby Song', from *Jack Straw's Castle* by Thom Gunn, published by Faber and Faber Ltd; Marilyn Hacker, 'To Iva, Two and a Half', from *Taking Notice* by Marilyn Hacker. Copyright © 1976, 1978, 1979, 1980 by Marilyn Hacker. Reprinted by permission of Frances Collin, Literary Agent. All copying, including electronic, or re-distribution of this text, is expressly forbidden.; Seamus Heaney, 'A Pillowed Head', from *Seeing Things* by Seamus Heaney, published by Faber and Faber Ltd; Selima Hill, extract from 'The Accumulation of Small Acts of Kindness', from *Gloria: Selected Poems* (Bloodaxe Books, 2008); Kathleen Jamie, 'The Barrel

permission of SLL/Sterling Lord Literistic, Inc. Copyright by Anne Sexton; Penelope Shuttle, 'The Conceiving', from *Selected Poems*, 1998, published by Oxford Poets; Anne Stevenson, 'The Victory' and 'The Spirit Is Too Blunt an Instrument', from *Poems 1955–2000* (Bloodaxe Books, 2005); Wisława Szymborska, 'The Story So Far', trans. Colette Bryce, by permission of Colette Bryce; C. K. Williams, 'The Rampage', from *Collected Poems* (Bloodaxe Books, 2006); Hugo Williams, 'Sugar Daddy', from *Collected Poems* by Hugo Williams, published by Faber and Faber Ltd.

Introduction

Birth may be one of life's central events, but, unlike love or death, it is not – or not yet – one of poetry's central subjects. The majority of our canonical poets are silent on the subject of babies, or use them only as a way of contemplating their own childhoods or to philosophize about innocence. More, science and obstetrics have so radically changed our views of pregnancy and birth as to render many poems from previous centuries emotionally unrecognizable: when Anne Bradstreet considered birth, for example, she contemplated, as indeed was only practical, her own death; in the nineteenth century, the numberless early deaths of infants led not only to numberless elegies but to a desperate, apologetic sentimentality about living children that now seems indigestibly maudlin; most recently, ultrasound has changed pregnancy from a mystery to a story with pictures familiar to us all – indeed, it has virtually spawned its own poetic genre. Feminism has had a huge impact both on women's freedom to write and in lifting taboos on speaking about the body: it is hard now to imagine the shocking impact of 'In Celebration of My Uterus' when Anne Sexton first started reading it in sixties America.

For these reasons, the presiding spirits of this book are twentieth- and twenty-first-century women: Frances Cornford, E. J. Scovell, Kathleen Jamie, Sharon Olds. Women dominate the first half of the volume, which is about conception, pregnancy and birth – though it is interesting to see these subjects becoming available to leading contemporary male poets too. In the second half of the volume, the voices of men and poets from the past become equally important. When it comes to blessing and naming our children, hoping for their futures, and remembering our childhoods through theirs, it seems that very little has changed since Samuel Taylor Coleridge contemplated his son Hartley in his cradle in 'Frost at Midnight', or since Hartley himself, whose work is extraordinarily full of children, promised his god-child unconditional love:

> We love, because we love thee, little lad,
> And pray thou may'st be good – because we love thee.

The Story So Far

The world is never ready
for the coming of a child.

Our ships have yet to return from Vinland.
We have still to cross St Gothard's Pass
and to dodge the guards at the sands of Thor.
We must sneak through the sewers
to the very heart of Warsaw,
wait for Minister Fouché's fall,
get a message to Harald, the king.
Only in a place like Acapulco
could we begin again.

We've run out of water, bandages, luck.
We have neither trucks nor the Ming's support.
We'd be fools to suppose this emaciated horse
would ever be enough to bribe the sheriff.
Still no word on the prisoners.
We'll have to secure us a warmer cave
for the freeze, and a man who can speak Harari.

Who can we trust these days in Nineveh?
What will be the next Prince-Cardinal decree?
Whose are the names still listed in Beria's files?
The wires quiver with the news
that Karol the Hammer will strike at dawn.
Come on, let us appease Cheops,
let's give ourselves up,

change our faith.
We can always pretend to be friendly with the Doge
and deny all links with the wild Kwabes.

It's time to build and light the fires,
to loosen the knots in the yurta's straps.
Let's put in the call to Grandma at Zabierzuw.

May delivery be easy.
May the child gain weight and be well.
Let her be happy from time to time
and learn, in time, to leap the abysses.
May her heart be true and strong,
and her mind sharp – may it range far

but not so far
as to see into the future.
God preserve her
from this gift.

Wisława Szymborska
Translated by Colette Bryce

Juice
Conception

Juice

My parents were virgins
At 22 – a bit much, even back then.
Dad was taken for a ladies' man in the halls of
    residence,
It's true. But he only went to ladies to eat
Because he was living on a student grant.
At first he went round to Mum's to eat, too.
And when they started talking about their
    wedding at college
Someone left a book out for Mum:
On becoming a real woman.
But Mum chucked it away without reading it.
Making me was terrible.
Making me was strange.
Making me was painful.
Making me was funny.
And I absorbed:
Life is terrible.
Life is strange.
Life is painful.
Life is very funny.

Vera Pavlova
Translated by Sasha Dugdale

The Conception

In the white sheets I gave you
everything I am capable of –
   at the wrong time
of the month we opened
   to the conception,

you were dewed like a plum
   when at two a.m.
you reached under the bed
for a drink of water adrift
   in yesterday's clothes,

   our sheets were a rope
caught between our thighs,
   we might easily have died
   but we kept on climbing.

HELEN DUNMORE

The Planned Child

I hated the fact that they had planned me, she had taken
a cardboard out of his shirt from the laundry
as if sliding the backbone up out of his body,
and made a chart of the month and put
her temperature on it, rising and falling,
to know the day to make me – I would have
liked to have been conceived in heat,
in haste, by mistake, in love, in sex,
not on cardboard, the little *x* on the
rising line that did not fall again.

But when a friend was pouring wine
dark as maroon clay, and said
that I seem to have been a child who had been wanted,
I took the wine against my lips
as if my mouth were moving along
that valved wall in my mother's body, she was
bearing down, and then breathing from the mask, and then
bearing down, pressing me out into
the world that was not enough for her without me in it,
not the moon, the sun, Orion
cartwheeling across the dark, not
the earth, the sea – none of it
was enough, for her, without me.

SHARON OLDS

Roulette

Put it on a number, you smile, catching
me chart the pattern of the last ten goes.
Funny to end up here, at the casino,
the first night of this break we can't afford,
but need, we feel, before the IVF.

Nine of the last ten being red, I plump
for black: first two chips (red though, damn), then four,
(fuck, red again), now six (no prizes), then –
all in – our last eight chips, and watch the ball
race round and round the wall of the roulette wheel,

so shiny I can see you, smaller,
in that nightshirt the same cut as your dress,
emerging from the bathroom one month hence
to show me, by your look, that everything
is lost, or else not lost at all, but yes, but yes . . .

RICHARD MEIER

The Train

The train came through the station as we were leaving.
Snaking between the platforms and out again
Leaving behind the village, the road to the estate,
The sealskin car park, lined with trees.

At that moment the lights came on.
It was dusk and a hundred radios announced the news.
Bulbs lit up as women struggled indoors.
Car doors click-locked; TV pictures filled screens.

As the evening rose in warm kitchens
The train slipped through the dusk,
Through hours, towns and suburbs,
Tying lives together like odd bits of string.

We made love in the front bedroom,
Washed and made a cup of tea.
The streetlamp outside was ticking softly.
Somewhere down the line you smiled.

SASHA DUGDALE

The Barrel Annunciation

I blame the pail
set under our blocked kitchen rhone
which I slopped across the yard

and hoisted to the butt's
oaken rim seven
or nine times in that spring storm;

so plunging rain upon the rain
held in its deep hooped belly
and triggering, unwittingly

without a counter-act of spillage,
some arcane craft laid
like a tripwire or snare,

lore, which, if I'd known,
would have dismissed as dupery
– a crone's trick,

sold to the barren at her cottage door
for a dull coin
or a skirt-length of homespun.

KATHLEEN JAMIE

The Conceiving

for Zoe

Now
you are in the ark of my blood
in the river of my bones
in the woodland of my muscles
in the ligaments of my hair
in the wit of my hands
in the smear of my shadow
in the armada of my brain
under the stars of my skull
in the arms of my womb
Now you are here
you worker in the gold of flesh

PENELOPE SHUTTLE

In Celebration of My Uterus

Everyone in me is a bird.
I am beating all my wings.
They wanted to cut you out
but they will not.
They said you were immeasurably empty
but you are not.
They said you were sick unto dying
but they were wrong.
You are singing like a school girl.
You are not torn.

Sweet weight,
In celebration of the woman I am
and of the soul of the woman I am
and of the central creature and its delight
I sing for you. I dare to live.
Hello, spirit. Hello, cup.
Fasten, cover. Cover that does contain.
Hello to the soil of the fields.
Welcome, roots.

Each cell has a life.
There is enough here to please a nation.
It is enough that the populace own these goods.
Any person, any commonwealth would say of it,
'It is good this year that we may plant again
and think forward to a harvest.
A blight had been forecast and has been cast out.'

Many women are singing together of this:
One is in a shoe factory cursing the machine,
one is at the aquarium tending a seal,
one is dull at the wheel of her Ford,
one is at the toll gate collecting,
one is tying the cord of a calf in Arizona,
one is straddling a cello in Russia,
one is shifting pots on the stove in Egypt,
one is painting her bedroom walls moon color,
one is dying but remembering a breakfast,
one is stretching on her mat in Thailand,
one is wiping the ass of her child,
one is staring out the window of a train
in the middle of Wyoming and one is
anywhere and some are everywhere and all
seem to be singing, although some can not
sing a note.

Sweet weight,
in celebration of the woman I am
let me carry a ten-foot scarf,
let me drum for the nineteen-year-olds,
let me carry bowls for the offering
(if that is my part).
Let me study the cardiovascular tissue,
let me examine the angular distance of meteors,
let me suck on the stems of flowers
(if that is my part).
Let me make certain tribal figures
(if that is my part).
For this thing the body needs
let me sing

for the supper,
for the kissing,
for the correct
yes.

ANNE SEXTON

Scan at 8 Weeks

The white receiver
slides up my vagina,

I turn and you've come,
though I'm much too old for this
and you're much too young.

That's the baby
says the radiographer.
You are eight millimetres long
and pulsing,

bright in the centre of my much-used womb
which to my astonishment
still looks immaculate.

You are all heart,
I watch you tick and tick

and wonder
what you will come to,

will this be our only encounter
in the white gallery of ultrasound

or are you staying?
One day will we talk about this

moment when I first saw your spaceship
far off, heading for home?

HELEN DUNMORE

The Keep

Sleep she on the eastern side,
holding a dream intact.

Sleep he turned to the west,
nursing a cracked rib.

Spine to spine, night over
turn they and face, make good

in the bed's trench. None break,
one keep in the bone crib.

SIMON ARMITAGE

Solstice

To whom do I talk, an unborn thou,
sleeping in a bone creel.

Look what awaits you:
stars, milk-bottles, frost
on a broken outhouse roof.

Let's close the door,
and rearrange
the dark red curtain.

Can you tell the days are opening,
admit a touch more light,
just a touch more?

KATHLEEN JAMIE

This New Heart

Pregnancy

Heartsong

I heard your heartbeat.
It flew out into the room, a startled bird
whirring high and wild.

I stopped breathing to listen
so high and fast it would surely race itself
down and fall

but it held strong, light
vibrant beside the slow deep booming
my old heart suddenly audible.

Out of the union that holds us separate
you've sent me a sound like a name.
Now I know you'll be born.

JENI COUZYN

Ultrasound

for Duncan

Oh whistle and I'll come to ye,
my lad, my wee shilpit ghost
summonsed from tomorrow.

Second sight,
a seer's mothy flicker,
an inner sprite:

this is what I see
with eyes closed;
a keek-aboot among secrets.

If Pandora
could have scanned
her dark box,

and kept it locked –
this ghoul's skull, punched eyes
is tiny Hope's,

hauled silver-quick
in a net of sound,
then, for pity's sake, lowered.

KATHLEEN JAMIE

from The Prince of the Quotidian

Only a few weeks ago, the sonogram of Jean's womb
resembled nothing so much
as a satellite map of Ireland:

now the image
is so well-defined we can make out not only a hand
but a thumb;

on the road to Spiddal, a woman hitching a ride;
a gladiator in his net, passing judgement on the crowd.

PAUL MULDOON

You're

Clownlike, happiest on your hands,
Feet to the stars, and moon-skulled,
Gilled like a fish. A common-sense
Thumbs-down on the dodo's mode.
Wrapped up in yourself like a spool,
Trawling your dark as owls do.
Mute as a turnip from the Fourth
Of July to All Fools' Day,
O high-riser, my little loaf.

Vague as fog and looked for like mail.
Farther off than Australia.
Bent-backed Atlas, our traveled prawn.
Snug as a bud and at home
Like a sprat in a pickle jug.
A creel of eels, all ripples.
Jumpy as a Mexican bean.
Right, like a well-done sum.
A clean slate, with your own face on.

Sylvia Plath

24

from To a Little Invisible Being Who Is
Expected Soon to Become Visible

For thee the nurse prepares her lulling songs,
The eager matrons count the lingering day;
But far the most thy anxious parent longs
On thy soft cheek a mother's kiss to lay.

She only asks to lay her burden down,
That her glad arms that burden may resume;
And nature's sharpest pangs her wishes crown,
That free thee living from thy living tomb.

She longs to fold to her maternal breast
Part of herself, yet to herself unknown;
To see and to salute the stranger guest,
Fed with her life through many a tedious moon.

Come, reap thy rich inheritance of love!
Bask in the fondness of a Mother's eye!
Nor wit nor eloquence her heart shall move
Like the first accents of thy feeble cry.

Haste, little captive, burst thy prison doors!
Launch on the living world, and spring to light!
Nature for thee displays her various stores,
Opens her thousand inlets of delight.

If charmèd verse or muttered prayers had power
With favouring spells to speed thee on thy way,
Anxious I'd bid my beads each passing hour,
Till thy wished smile thy mother's pangs o'erpay.

ANNA LAETITIA BARBAULD

Footling

This I don't believe: rather than take a header
off the groyne
and into the ground swell,
yea verily, the ground swell of life,

she shows instead her utter
disregard – part diffidence, but mostly scorn –
for what lies behind the great sea-wall
and what knocks away at the great sea-cliff;

though she's been in training all spring and summer
and swathed herself in fat
and Saran-

Wrap like an old-time Channel swimmer,
she's now got cold feet
and turned in on herself, the phantom 'a' in Cesarian.

PAUL MULDOON

For a Child Expected

Our baby was to be the living sign of our joy,
Restore to each the other's lost infancy;
To a painter's pillaging eye
Poet's coiled hearing, add the heart we might earn
By the help of love; all that our passion would yield
We put to planning our child.

The world flowed in; whatever we liked we took:
For its hair, the gold curls of the November oak
We saw on our walk;
Snowberries that make a Milky Way in the wood
For its tender hands; calm screen of the frozen flood
For our care of its childhood.

But the birth of a child is an uncontrollable glory;
Cat's cradle of hopes will hold no living baby,
Long though it lay quietly.
And when our baby stirs and struggles to be born
It compels humility: what we began
Is now its own.

For 'as the sun that shines through glass
So Jesus in His Mother was'.
Therefore every human creature,
Since it shares in His nature,
In candle-gold passion or white
Sharp star should show its own way of light.
May no parental dread or dream

Darken our darling's early beam:
May she grow to her right powers
Unperturbed by passion of ours.

ANNE RIDLER

Prayer

Our baby's heart, on the sixteen-week scan
was a fluttering bird, held in cupped hands.

I thought of St Kevin, hands opened in prayer
and a bird of the hedgerow nesting there,

and how he'd borne it, until the young had flown
– and I prayed: this new heart must outlive my own.

KATHLEEN JAMIE

To Enter That Rhythm Where the Self Is Lost

Birth

To Enter That Rhythm Where
the Self Is Lost

To enter that rhythm where the self is lost,
where breathing: heartbeat: and the subtle music
of their relation make our dance, and hasten
us to the moment when all things become
magic, another possibility.
That blind moment, midnight, when all sight
begins, and the dance itself is all our breath,
and we ourselves the moment of life and death.
Blinded; but given now another saving,
the self as vision, at all times perceiving,
all arts all senses being languages,
delivered of will, being transformed in truth –
for life's sake surrendering moment and images,
writing the poem; in love making; bringing to birth.

MURIEL RUKEYSER

The Funniest Bit

The funniest bit was giving birth.
Off you go, muttered the midwife
And waved her hand vaguely
Somewhere along the corridor.
I grabbed my bump and went.
And went and went until suddenly: a mirror,
And in the mirror a belly
In a shirt to the navel,
On thin, trembling
Lilac legs –
I laughed for about five minutes.
Five minutes later I gave birth.

VERA PAVLOVA
Translated by Sasha Dugdale

A Circus

I doubt anyone would've blinked if a ringmaster
marched in among us and this blarneying broadcaster
raised a megaphone to his lips announcing
another highlight of the Greatest Show on Earth
along with the likes of the ball-bouncing,
baby-blubber seals; the hoop-leaping lemurs of mirth;
the tremendous, stupendous fandango of horses;
highflying doctors; funambulist nurses;
and all the farraginous farrago of this Earth,
not excluding me, the whistle-blowing clown,
the huffing and puffing red-faced Bozo father
of fathers, wearing a lugubrious frown,
cracking side-splitting sideshow banter
and flat-footed jokes, a sidekick to your mother.
The whole death-defying show spun out of order
as a drum-roll hailed you; the debonair,
high-flying, dare-devil, god of the air,
none other than the Cannonball Kid himself
shot from the dilatory, dilative distaff
opening of your ma, the human cannon herself,
lit a little over nine months ago by your father.
Your grey jump suit was smeared with bloody gauze
as you landed in the hand-net of nurse and doctor;
the whole show agape in the pause before applause.

GREG DELANTY

35

The Birth

Seven o'clock. The seventh day of the seventh month of
    the year.
No sooner have I got myself up in lime-green scrubs,
a sterile cap and mask,
and taken my place at the head of the table

than the windlass-women ply their shears
and gralloch-grub
for a footling foot, then, warming to their task,
haul into the inestimable

realm of apple-blossoms and chanterelles and damsons
    and eel-spears
and foxes and the general hubbub
of inkies and jennets and Kickapoos with their lemniscs
or peekaboo-quiffs of Russian sable

and tallow-unctuous vernix, into the realm
of the widgeon – the 'whew' or 'yellow-poll', not the
    'zuizin' –

Dorothy Aoife Korelitz Muldoon: I watch through
    floods of tears
as they give her a quick rub-a-dub
and whisk
her off to the nursery, then check their staple-guns
    for staples.

PAUL MULDOON

St Bride's

for Freya

So this is women's work: folding
and unfolding, be it linen or a selkie-
skin tucked behind a rock. Consider

the hare in jizzen: her leveret's ears
flat as the mizzen of a ship
entering a bottle. A thread's trick;

adders uncoil into spring. Feathers
of sunlight, glanced from a butterknife
quiver on the ceiling,

and a last sharp twist for the shoulders
delivers my daughter, the placenta
following, like a fist of purple kelp.

KATHLEEN JAMIE

The Language of the Brag

I have wanted excellence in the knife-throw,
I have wanted to use my exceptionally strong and
    accurate arms
and my straight posture and quick electric muscles
to achieve something at the center of a crowd,
the blade piercing the bark deep,
the haft slowly and heavily vibrating like the cock.

I have wanted some epic use for my excellent body,
some heroism, some American achievement
beyond the ordinary for my extraordinary self,
magnetic and tensile, I have stood by the sandlot
and watched the boys play.

I have wanted courage, I have thought about fire
and the crossing of waterfalls, I have dragged around

my belly big with cowardice and safety,
my stool black with iron pills,
my huge breasts oozing mucus,
my legs swelling, my hands swelling,
my face swelling and darkening, my hair
falling out, my inner sex
stabbed again and again with terrible pain like a knife.
I have lain down.

I have lain down and sweated and shaken
and passed blood and feces and water and

slowly alone in the center of a circle I have
passed the new person out
and they have lifted the new person free of the act
and wiped the new person free of that
language of blood like praise all over the body.

I have done what you wanted to do, Walt Whitman,
Allen Ginsberg, I have done this thing,
I and the other women this exceptional
act with the exceptional heroic body,
this giving birth, this glistening verb,
and I am putting my proud American boast
right here with the others.

SHARON OLDS

The Victory

I thought you were my victory
though you cut me like a knife
when I brought you out of my body
into your life.

Tiny antagonist, gory,
blue as a bruise. The stains
of your cloud of glory
bled from my veins.

How can you dare, blind thing,
blank insect eyes?
You barb the air. You sting
with bladed cries.

Snail! Scary knot of desires!
Hungry snarl! Small son.
Why do I have to love you?
How have you won?

ANNE STEVENSON

Well Done, My Lord
Thanksgiving

from Demeter and Persephone

Faint as a climate-changing bird that flies
All night across the darkness, and at dawn
Falls on the threshold of her native land,
And can no more, thou camest, O my child,
Led upward by the God of ghosts and dreams . . .

ALFRED, LORD TENNYSON

from Ode on Intimations of Immortality

Our birth is but a sleep and a forgetting:
The Soul that rises with us, our life's Star,
Hath had elsewhere its setting,
And cometh from afar:
Not in entire forgetfulness,
And not in utter nakedness,
But trailing clouds of glory do we come
From God, who is our home:

WILLIAM WORDSWORTH

from The Salutation

From dust I rise,
And out of nothing now awake;
These brighter regions which salute mine eyes,
A gift from God I take.
The earth, the seas, the light, the lofty skies,
The sun and stars are mine; if these I prize.

A stranger here,
Strange things doth meet, strange glory see;
Strange treasures lodged in this fair world appear,
Strange all and new to me;
But that they mine should be, who nothing was,
That strangest is of all, yet brought to pass.

THOMAS TRAHERNE

Birth

The rain is over.

Still it sings in my ears
from the roofs and the trees.
And covers my head
with a blue veil.

Well done, my Lord,
the child is caught in your net.
Now I'll put leaf against leaf
to see how leaf covers leaf
and the raindrops connect.
And I'll call swallows
to the wedding from my heaven,
I'll crown all my windows with flower-pots.

Well done, my Lord,
the child is caught in your net.
I open my eyes,
my land's very wide

and all of it
one flower stem
and green!

Oh Lord, how close we've been!

AMIR GILBOA
Translated by Shirley Kaufman

Hello

The First Weeks

Thaw

When we brought you home in a taxi
through the steel-grey thaw
after the coldest week in memory
– even the river sealed itself –
it was I, hardly breathing,
who came through the passage to our yard
welcoming our simplest things:
a chopping block, the frost-
split lintels; and though it meant a journey
through darkening snow,
arms laden with you in a blanket,
I had to walk to the top of the garden,
to touch, in a complicit homage of equals, the spiral
trunks of our plum trees, the moss,
the robin's roost in the holly.
Leaning back on the railway wall,
I tried to remember;
but even my footprints were being erased
and the rising stars of Orion
denied what I knew: that as we were
hurled on a trolley through swing doors to theatre
they'd been there, aligned on the ceiling, ablaze with
    concern
for that difficult giving,
before we were two, from my one.

KATHLEEN JAMIE

from The First Year

All deeds undone, all words unsaid,
Null as a flower, sleep on my bed.
None to compare you with, for you
Are type and inmost form of New.

Darkness your home – what need at all
To be cast out, washed, wrapped in a shawl;
And soon, the same and not the same,
Be bent to attributes and name?

What should you do, new born, but fall
Asleep, in sleep disclosing all?
What can you do but sleep, an hour from birth,
Lacking an answer yet to give to earth?

E. J. SCOVELL

'This lunar beauty'

This lunar beauty
Has no history
Is complete and early;
If beauty later
Bear any feature
It had a lover
And is another.

This like a dream
Keeps other time
And daytime is
The loss of this;
For time is inches
And the heart's changes
Where ghost has haunted
Lost and wanted.

But this was never
A ghost's endeavour
Nor finished this,
Was ghost at ease;
And till it pass
Love shall not near

The sweetness here
Nor sorrow take
His endless look.

W. H. AUDEN

Cradle Song for Asher

When they cut your birth cord yesterday
it was I who drifted away.

Now I hear your name (in Hebrew, 'blest')
as yet another release of ballast

and see, beyond your wicker
gondola, camp-fires, cities, whole continents flicker.

PAUL MULDOON

Hel*lo*

Hel*lo* there, Biscuit! You're a better-looking broad
By much than, and your sister's dancing up & down.
'I just gave one mighty Push'
your mother says, and we are all in business.

I thought your mother might powder my knuckles
gript at one point, with wild eyes on my tie
'Don't move!' and then the screams began,
they wheeled her off, and we are all in business.

I wish I knew what business (son) we're in
I can't wait seven weeks to see her grin
I'm not myself, we are all changing here
direction *and* velocity, to accommodate you, dear.

JOHN BERRYMAN

A Pillowed Head

Matutinal. Mother-of-pearl
Summer come early. Slashed carmines
And washed milky blues.

To be first on the road.
Up with the ground-mists and pheasants.
To be older and grateful

That this time you too were half-grateful
The pangs had begun – prepared
And clear-headed, foreknowing

The trauma, entering on it
With full consent of the will.
(The first time, dismayed and arrayed

In your cut-off white cotton gown,
You were more bride than earth-mother
Up on the stirrup-rigged bed,

Who were self-possessed now
To the point of a walk on the pier
Before you checked in.)

And then later on I half-fainted
When the little slapped palpable girl
Was handed to me; but as usual

Came to in two wide-open eyes
That had been dawned into farther
Than ever, and had outseen the last

Of all those mornings of waiting
When your domed brow was one long held silence
And the dawn chorus anything but.

SEAMUS HEANEY

Her First Week

She was so small I would scan the crib a half-second
to find her, face-down in a corner, limp
as something gently flung down, or fallen
from some sky an inch above the mattress. I would
tuck her arm along her side
and slowly turn her over. She would tumble
over part by part, like a load
of damp laundry in the dryer, I'd slip
a hand in, under her neck,
slide the other under her back,
and evenly lift her up. Her little bottom
sat in my palm, her chest contained
the puckered, moire sacs, and her neck –
I was afraid of her neck, once I almost
thought I heard it quietly snap,
I looked at her and she swivelled her slate
eyes and looked at me. It was in
my care, the creature of her spine, like the first
chordate, as if the history
of the vertebrate had been placed in my hands.
Every time I checked, she was still
with us – someday, there would be a human
race. I could not see it in her eyes,
but when I fed her, gathered her
like a loose bouquet to my side and offered

the breast, greyish-white, and struck with
minuscule scars like creeks in sunlight, I
felt she was serious, I believed she was willing to stay.

SHARON OLDS

Sea Urchin

Between my breast
and cupped hand,
your head
rests as tenderly
as once I may
have freighted
water, or drawn
treasure, whole
from a rockpool
with no premonition
of when next I find one
cast up
broken.

Kathleen Jamie

Overhanging Cloud

This morning the overhanging clouds are piecrust,
milelong Luxor Temples based on rich runny ooze;
my old life settles down into the archives.
It's strange having a child today, though common,
adding our further complication to
intense fragility.
Clouds go from dull to dazzle all the morning;
we have not grown as our child did in the womb,
met Satan like Milton going blind in London;
it's enough to wake without old fears,
and watch the needle-fire of the first light
bombarding off your eyelids harmlessly.
By ten the bedroom is sultry. You have double-breathed;
we are many, our bed smells of hay.

ROBERT LOWELL

Waking with Russell

Whatever the difference is, it all began
the day we woke up face-to-face like lovers
and his four-day-old smile dawned on him again,
possessed him, till it would not fall or waver;
and I pitched back not my old hard-pressed grin
but his own smile, or one I'd rediscovered.
Dear son, I was *mezzo del cammin*
and the true path was as lost to me as ever
when you cut in front and lit it as you ran.
See how the true gift never leaves the giver:
returned and redelivered, it rolled on
until the smile poured through us like a river.
How fine, I thought, this waking amongst men!
I kissed your mouth and pledged myself forever.

DON PATERSON

February

To the heap of nappies
carried from the automatic
in a red plastic basket

to the hanging out, my mouth
crowded with pegs;
to the notched prop

hoisting the wash,
a rare flight of swans,
hills still courying snow;

to spring's hint sailing
the westerly, snowdrops
sheltered by rowans –

to the day of St Bride, the first
sweet-wild weeks of your life
I willingly surrender.

KATHLEEN JAMIE

Infant Sorrow, Infant Joy
The First Months

Morning Song

Love set you going like a fat gold watch.
The midwife slapped your footsoles, and your bald cry
Took its place among the elements.

Our voices echo, magnifying your arrival. New statue.
In a drafty museum, your nakedness
Shadows our safety. We stand round blankly as walls.

I'm no more your mother
Than the cloud that distills a mirror to reflect its own slow
Effacement at the wind's hand.

All night your moth-breath
Flickers among the flat pink roses. I wake to listen:
A far sea moves in my ear.

One cry, and I stumble from bed, cow-heavy and floral
In my Victorian nightgown.
Your mouth opens clean as a cat's. The window square

Whitens and swallows its dull stars. And now you try
Your handful of notes;
The clear vowels rise like balloons.

SYLVIA PLATH

Patrick I

Patrick, I cannot write
such poems for you as a father might
coming upon your smile,

your mouth, half sucking, half sleeping,
your tears shaken from your eyes like sparklers
break up the nightless weeks of your life:

lightheaded, I go to the kitchen
and cook breakfast, aching as you grow hungry.
Mornings are plain as the pages
of books in sedentary schooldays.

If I were eighty and lived next door
hanging my pale chemises on the porch
would I envy or pity my neighbour?

Polished and still as driftwood
she stands smoothing her dahlias;

liquid, leaking,
I cup the baby's head to my shoulder:

the child's a boy and will not share
one day these obstinate, exhausted mornings.

HELEN DUNMORE

from The Accumulation of Small Acts
of Kindness

Whenever a child is born, a woman is wasted.
We do not quite belong to ourselves.
Crushing all the hollyhocks with teddies,
the wa-wa babies stumble: 'Lift me up!'

You see, it is so lonely I get serious.
Dream of a dream and shadow of a shade.
'The writer's instinct is essentially heartless.'
The wa-wa babies burst into floods of tears.

SELIMA HILL

71

Young Mothers II

She is all eyes and ears for damage.
In her loose shirt her breasts like white wolves' heads
sway and snarl. She does not trust anyone.
They have torn her soul out of her body and said
the child is the other one.

Always a new baby to take her place,
and now she's a lady-in-waiting again
to a queen. Out of her mother's house
she has fallen into her daughter's.
She cooks little things in hot fat,
she pushes the carriage filled with a raw roast,
she stands outside a window and watches a childless
    couple
fucking in the resinous light of a fire
without interruption.

SHARON OLDS

The Rampage

a baby got here once who before
he was all the way out and could already feel the hindu
pain inside him and the hebrew and the iliad
decided he was never going to stop crying no matter what
until they did something he wasn't going
to turn the horror
off in their fat sentences
and in the light bulb how much murder to get light
and in the walls agony agony for the bricks for the glaze
he was going to keep screaming
until they made death little like he was
and loved him too and sent
him back to undo all this
and it happened
he kept screaming he scared them he saw them
filling with womblight again like stadiums
he saw the tears sucked back into the story the smiles
opening like sandwiches
so he stopped
and looked up and said all right
it's better now
I'm hungry now I want just to sleep
and they let him

C. K. WILLIAMS

Infant Sorrow

My mother groan'd! my father wept.
Into the dangerous world I leapt:
Helpless, naked, piping loud:
Like a fiend hid in a cloud.

Struggling in my father's hands,
Striving against my swadling bands,
Bound and weary I thought best
To sulk upon my mother's breast.

WILLIAM BLAKE

from To —— (Isabella Wordsworth)
Upon the Birth of Her First-Born Child,
March 1833

Like a shipwreck'd Sailor tost
By rough waves on a perilous coast,
Lies the Babe, in helplessness
And in tenderest nakedness,
Flung by labouring nature forth
Upon the mercies of the earth.
Can its eyes beseech? No more
Than the hands are free to implore:
Voice but serves for one brief cry,
Plaint was it? Or prophecy
Of sorrow that will surely come?
Omen of man's grievous doom.

WILLIAM WORDSWORTH
(after Lucretius)

Baby Song

From the private ease of Mother's womb
I fall into the lighted room.

Why don't they simply put me back
Where it is warm and wet and black?

But one thing follows on another.
Things were different inside Mother.

Padded and jolly I would ride
The perfect comfort of her inside.

They tuck me in a rustling bed
– I lie there, raging, small, and red.

I may sleep soon, I may forget,
But I won't forget that I regret.

A rain of blood poured round her womb,
But all time roars outside this room.

THOM GUNN

Cradle Song at Twilight

The child not yet is lulled to rest.
Too young a nurse, the slender Night
So laxly holds him to her breast
That throbs with flight.

He plays with her, and will not sleep.
For other playfellows she sighs;
An unmaternal fondness keep
Her alien eyes.

ALICE MEYNELL

Hushabye, Baby

Hushabye, baby, thy cradle is green,
Father's a nobleman, thy Mother's a Queen,
Betty's a lady and wears a gold ring,
And Johnny's a drummer and drums for the King.

ANON.

Sweet and Low

Sweet and low, sweet and low,
  Wind of the western sea,
Low, low, breathe and blow,
  Wind of the western sea!
Over the rolling waters go,
Come from the dying moon, and blow,
  Blow him again to me;
While my little one, while my pretty one, sleeps.

Sleep and rest, sleep and rest,
  Father will come to thee soon;
Rest, rest, on mother's breast,
  Father will come to thee soon;
Father will come to his babe in the nest,
Silver sails all out of the west
  Under the silver moon:
Sleep, my little one, sleep, my pretty one, sleep.

ALFRED, LORD TENNYSON

Bairnsang

Wee toshie man,
gean tree and rowan
gif ye could staun
yer feet wad lichtsome tread
granite an saun,
but ye cannae yet staun
sae maun courie tae ma airm
an greetna, girna, Gretna Green
Peedie wee lad
saumon, siller haddie
gin ye could rin
ye'd rin richt easy-strang
ower causey an carse,
but ye cannae yet rin
sae maun jist courie in
and fashna, fashna, Macrahanish Sand

Bonny wee boy
peeswheep an whaup
gin ye could sing, yer sang
wad be caller
as a lauchin mountain burn
but ye cannae yet sing
sae maun courie tae ma hert
an grieve nat at aa, Ainster an Crail

My ain tottie bairn
sternie an lift

gin ye could daunce, yer daunce
wad be that o life itsel,
but ye cannae yet daunce
sae maun courie in my erms
and sleep, saftly sleep, Unst and Yell

KATHLEEN JAMIE

from Amantium Irae

In going to my naked bed as one that would have slept,
I heard a wife sing to her child, that long before had
  wept.
She sighèd sore and sung full sweet, to bring the babe
  to rest,
That would not cease, but crièd still, in sucking at her
  breast.
She was full weary of her watch, and grievèd with her
  child,
She rockèd it, and rated it, till that on her it smiled.
Then did she say 'Now have I found, this proverb true
  to prove,
The falling out of faithful friendes, renewing is of love.'

RICHARD EDWARDES

Mother to Child Asleep

These tiny, fringed eyes
Must look on all that dies;
In some strange dawn with bleeding tears perceive
This house they now believe
Coeval with its dome
Of arching sky, this home
Which an unending tabernacle seems,
Dissolve like dreams –
This tree-tall clock, that sempiternal door,
The table white for dinner, all no more.

Ah, though I might, no magic must be willed
On your vexed waters, vexed when mine are stilled.
On that strange morning you must sail alone,
My utterly-sleeping own.

FRANCES CORNFORD

Dawn

Of your hand I could say this
a bird poised mid-air in flight
as delicate and smooth.

Of your mouth
a foxglove in its taking
without edges or hurt.

This of your ear
a tiny sea-horse, immortal
sporting in white waves

and of your eye
a place where no one could hide
nothing lurk.

Of your cupped flesh
smooth in my palm
an agate on the sea-shore

of your back and belly
that they command kisses.
And of your feet I would say

they are inquisitive and gay
as squirrels or birds
and so return to your hand

and begin my voyage
around your loveliness
again and yet again

as in my arms you lie sleeping.

JENI COUZYN

from The First Year

The days fail: night broods over afternoon:
And at my child's first drink beyond the night
Her skin is silver in the early light.
Sweet the grey morning and the raiders gone.

E. J. SCOVELL

High Office

Only the breastfeeder
knows the beauty of the ear,
only the breastfed
knows the collarbone's allure.
Only humans were given
an earlobe by the creator,
only in their collarbone
do they slightly resemble the birds,
in unbroken caresses
in night-time flying
to where, rocking the cradle
of cradles, the child is crying,
to where, on a pillow of air
sleepless, but pretending to sleep
rest the stars, his playthings.
And not one speaks.

VERA PAVLOVA
Translated by Sasha Dugdale

The New-Born Baby's Song

When I was twenty inches long.
I could not hear the thrushes' song;
The radiance of morning skies
Was most displeasing to my eyes.

For loving looks, caressing words,
I cared no more than sun or birds;
But I could bite my mother's breast,
And that made up for all the rest.

FRANCES CORNFORD

Little Feet

Little feet, too young and soft to walk,
Little lips, too young and pure to talk.

My baby has a mottled fist,
My baby has a neck in creases;
My baby kisses and is kissed,
For he's the very thing for kisses.

CHRISTINA ROSSETTI

from The First Year

The baby in her blue night-jacket, propped on hands
With head raised, coming out to day, has half-way
   sloughed
The bed-clothes, as a sea-lion, as a mermaid
Half sloughs the sea, rooted in sea, basking on strands.

Like a gentle coastal creature she looks round
At one who comes and goes the far side of her bars;
Firm in her place and lapped by blankets; here like tides
Familiar rise and care for her, our sounds.

E. J. SCOVELL

from A Mother to Her Waking Infant

Now in thy dazzling half-oped eye,
Thy curlèd nose and lip awry,
Thy up-hoist arms and noddling head,
And little chin with chrystal spread,
Poor helpless thing! what do I see,
   That I should sing of thee?

From thy poor tongue no accents come,
Which can but rub thy toothless gum;
Small understanding boasts thy face,
Thy shapeless limbs nor step nor grace;
A few short words thy feats may tell,
   And yet I love thee well.

When sudden wakes the bitter shriek,
And redder swells thy little cheek;
When rattled keys thy woes beguile,
And through the wet eye gleams the smile,
Still for thy weakly self is spent
   Thy little silly plaint.

But when thy friends are in distress,
Thou'lt laugh and chuckle ne'er the less;
Nor e'en with sympathy be smitten,
Though all are sad but thee and kitten;
Yet little varlet that thou art,
   Thou twitchest at the heart.

Thy rosy cheek so soft and warm;
Thy pinky hand and dimpled arm;
Thy silken locks that scantly peep,
With gold-tipped ends, where circles deep
Around thy neck in harmless grace
  So soft and sleekly hold their place,

Might harder hearts with kindness fill,
And gain our right good will . . .

Each passing clown bestows his blessing,
Thy mouth is worn with old wives' kissing:
E'en lighter looks the gloomy eye
Of surly sense, when thou art by;
And yet I think whoe'er they be;
  They love thee not like me.

JOANNA BAILLIE

Infant Joy

'I have no name –
I am but two days old.'
What shall I call thee?
'I happy am,
Joy is my name.'
Sweet joy befall thee!

Pretty joy!
Sweet joy but two days old –
Sweet joy I call thee.
Thou dost smile,
I sing the while –
Sweet joy befall thee!

WILLIAM BLAKE

from A Matter of Life and Death

His smiles are all largesse,
Need ask for no return,
Since give and take are meaningless
To one who gives by needing
And takes our love for granted
And grants a favour even by his greed.
The ballet of his twirling hands
His chirping and his loving sounds,
Perpetual expectation
Perpetual surprise –
Not a lifetime satisfies
For watching, everything he does
We wish him to do always.

ANNE RIDLER

Song for a Young Mother

There, there, you fit my lap
Like an acorn to its cup,
Your weight upon my arm
Is like a golden plum,
Like an apple in the hand
Or a stone on the ground.

As a bird in the fallow
scoops a shallow hollow
Where the earth's upward pressing
Answers egg and nestling
– Earth's mass and beginning
Of all their learning –

So you learn from my arm
You have substance and a house
So I learn from your birth
that I am not vague and wild
But as solid as my child
And as constant as the earth.

E. J. SCOVELL

Sugar Daddy

You do not look like me. I'm glad
England failed to colonize
Those black orchid eyes
With blue, the colour of sun-blindness.

Your eyes came straight to you
From your mother's Martinique
Great-grandmother. They look at me
Across this wide Atlantic

With an inborn feeling for my weaknesses.
Like loveletters, your little phoney grins
Come always just too late
To reward my passionate clowning.

I am here to be nice, clap hands, reflect
Your tolerance. I know what I'm for.
When you come home fifteen years from now
Saying you've smashed my car,

I'll feel the same. I'm blood brother,
Sugar-daddy, millionaire to you.
I want to buy you things.

I bought a garish humming top
And climbed into your pen like an ape
And pumped it till it screeched for you,
Hungry for thanks. Your lip

Trembled and you cried, You didn't need
My sinister grenade, something
Pushed out of focus at you, swaying
Violently. You owned it anyway

And the whole world it came from.
It was then I knew
I could only take things from you from now on.

I was the White Hunter,
Bearing cheap mirrors for the Chief.
You saw the giving-look coagulate in my eyes
And panicked for the trees.

HUGO WILLIAMS

from A Matter of Life and Death

Only in a lover's eyes
Shall I be so approved again;
Only the other side of pain
Can truth again be all I speak;
Or I again possess
A saint's hilarious carelessness.

ANNE RIDLER

from The First Year

As monks whose time is told by bells
Out of the strict hours see eternity,
I have watched your eternity, your world without
   beginning
These five months by the moon;

These days by the clock with their ritual repetitions,
Votive milk and early rising,
Plains of peace and fainting terrors,
And their meaning out of time.

For between one feed and another,
Your sleep's forgetting, your calms of waking
Have freed me to eternity
Like the sky through a little window-frame.

E. J. SCOVELL

29 April 1989

She's three months old now,
asleep at last for the afternoon.
I've got some time to myself again
but I don't know what to do.
Outside everything is greyish green and soggy
with endless Bremen-Spring drizzle.
I make a large pot of Assam tea
and search through the books
in my room, shift through my papers.
I'm not looking for anything, really,
just touching my favourite books.
I don't even know what I'm thinking,
but there's a rich round fullness
in the air
like living inside Beethoven's piano
on a day when he was
particularly energetic.

SUJATA BHATT

I Have Wished You Something
Namings and Blessings

The Spirit Is Too Blunt an Instrument

The spirit is too blunt an instrument
to have made this baby.
Nothing so unskilful as human passions
could have managed the intricate
exacting particulars: the tiny
blind bones with their manipulating tendons,
the knee and the knucklebones, the resilient
fine meshings of ganglia and vertebrae
in the chain of the difficult spine.

Observe the distinct eyelashes and sharp crescent
fingernails, the shell-like complexity
of the ear with its firm involutions
concentric in miniature to the minute
ossicles. Imagine the
infinitesimal capillaries, the flawless connections
of the lungs, the invisible neural filaments
through which the completed body
already answers to the brain.

Then name any passion or sentiment
possessed of the simplest accuracy.
No. No desire or affection could have done
with practice what habit
has done perfectly, indifferently,
through the body's ignorant precision.

It is left to the vagaries of the mind to invent
love and despair and anxiety
and their pain.

ANNE STEVENSON

Petal

Not a word I've used for anyone
before. And not particular, or funny,
like *molecule*, say, as your mother calls you.

Matilda, *petal* – little love-evoker –
I stand above your sleep-surrendered soul,
or else pull outsize grins you'll learn, I fear,

your father's not exactly famous for,
all teary, like a man half-cut,
but so, so sober. And completely yours.

RICHARD MEIER

Infant

In your frowning, fugitive days, small love,
your coracled, ecstatic nights,
possessed or at peace, hands clenched
on an unseen rope, or raised in blessing
like the Pope, as your white etched feet
tread sooty rooves of canal tunnels
or lie released, stretched North in sleep –

you seem to me an early saint, a Celt,
eyes fixed on a celestial light, patiently
setting the sextant straight
to follow your godsent map, now
braced against a baffling gale, now
becalmed, fingers barely sculling
through warm muddy tides.

Soon, you will make your way out
of this estuary country, leave
the low farms and fog banks, tack through
the brackish channels and long
reed-clogged rivulets, reach
the last turn, the salt air and river mouth,
the wide grey sea beyond it.

KATE CLANCHY

To a Ten Months' Child

for M.M.

Late arrival, no
One would think of blaming you
For hesitating so.

Who, setting his hand to knock
At a door so strange as this one,
Might not draw back?

Certainly, once admitted,
You will be made to feel
Like one of the invited.

Still, because you come
From so remote a kingdom,
You may feel out of place,

Tongue-tied and shy among
So many strangers, all
Babbling a strange tongue.

Well, that's no disgrace.
So might any person
So recently displaced,

Remembering the ocean,
So calm, so lately crossed.

DONALD JUSTICE

To Mistress Isabell Pennell

By Saint Mary, my lady,
Your mammy and your daddy
Brought forth a goodly babby!
My maiden Isabell,
Reflaring rosabelle,
The flagrant camomile;
The ruddy rosary,
The sovereign rosemary,
The pretty strawberry;
The columbine, the nepte,
The jeloflower well set,
The proper violet;
Enough, your colour
Is like the daisy flower
After the April shower;
Star of the morrow grey,
The blossom on the spray,
The freshest flower of May!
Maidenly demure,
Of womanhood the lure;
Wherefore, I make you sure,
It were an heavenly health,
It were an endless wealth,
A life for God himself,
To hear this nightingale
Among the birds small,
Warbling in the vale:

Dug, dug, jug, jug,
Good year and good luck,
With chuk, chuk, chuk, chuk.

JOHN SKELTON

Born Yesterday

for Sally Amis

Tightly-folded bud,
I have wished you something
None of the others would:
Not the usual stuff
About being beautiful,
Or running off a spring
Of innocence and love –
They will all wish you that,
And should it prove possible,
Well, you're a lucky girl.

But if it shouldn't, then
May you be ordinary;
Have, like other women,
An average of talents:
Not ugly, not good-looking,
Nothing uncustomary
To pull you off your balance,
That, unworkable itself,
Stops all the rest from working.
In fact, may you be dull –
If that is what a skilled,
Vigilant, flexible,
Unemphasized, enthralled
Catching of happiness is called.

PHILIP LARKIN

To C.F.H. on Her Christening-Day

Fair Caroline, I wonder what
You think of earth as a dwelling-spot,

And if you'd rather have come, or not?
Today has laid on you a name
That, though unasked for, you will claim
Lifelong, for love or praise or blame.

May chance and change impose on you
No heavier burthen than this new
Care-chosen one your future through!

Dear stranger here, the prayer is mine
That your experience may combine
Good things with glad . . . Yes, Caroline!

THOMAS HARDY

The God Child

I stood beside thee in the holy place
And saw the holy sprinkling on thy brow,
And was both bond and witness to the vow
Which own'd thy need, confirm'd thy claim of grace;
That sacred sign which time shall not efface
Declared thee His, to whom all angels bow,
Who bade the herald saint the rite allow
To the sole sinless of all Adam's race.
That was indeed an awful sight to see;
And oft, I fear, for what my love hath done,
As voucher of thy sweet communion
In thy sweet Saviour's blessed mystery.
Would I might give thee back, my little one,
But half the good that I have got from thee.

HARTLEY COLERIDGE

A Poet's Welcome to His Love-Begotten Daughter

The First Instance That Entitled Him
To The Venerable Appellation Of Father

Thou's welcome, wean! Mishanter fa' me,
If thoughts o' thee or yet thy mammie
Shall ever daunton me or awe me,
My sweet, wee lady,
Or if I blush when thou shalt ca' me
Tyta or daddie!

What tho' they ca' me fornicator,
An' tease my name in kintra clatter?
The mair they talk, I'm kend the better;
E'en let them clash!
An auld wife's tongue's a feckless matter
To gie ane fash.

Welcome, my bonnie, sweet, wee dochter!
Tho' ye come here a wee unsought for,
And tho' your comin I hae fought for
Baith kirk and queir;
Yet, by my faith, ye're no unwrought for
That I shall swear!

Sweet fruit o' monie a merry dint,
My funny toil is no a' tint:
Tho' thou cam to the warl' asklent,
Which fools may scoff at,
In my last plack thy part's be in't
The better half o't.

Tho' I should be the waur bestead,
Thou's be as braw and bienly clad,
And thy young years as nicely bred
Wi' education,
As onie brat o' wedlock's bed
In a' thy station.

Wee image o' my bonie Betty,
As fatherly I kiss and daut thee,
As dear and near my heart I set thee,
Wi' as guid will,
As a' the priests had seen me get thee
That's out o' Hell.

Gude grant that thou may ay inherit
Thy mither's looks an' gracefu' merit,
An' thy poor, worthless daddie's spirit
Without his failins!
'Twill please me mair to see thee heir it
Than stocket mailins.

And if thou be what I wad hae thee,
An' tak the counsel I shall gie thee,
I'll never rue my trouble wi' thee

The cost nor shame o't
But be a loving father to thee,
And brag the name o't.

ROBERT BURNS

To Ianthe

I love thee, Baby! for thine own sweetsake;
Those azure eyes, that faintly dimpled cheek,
Thy tender frame, so eloquently weak,
Love in the sternest heart of hate might wake;
But more when o'er thy fitful slumber bending
Thy mother folds thee to her wakeful heart,
Whilst love and pity, in her glances blending,
All that thy passive eyes can feel impart;
More, when some feeble lineaments of her,
Who bore thy weight beneath her spotless bosom,
As with deep love I read thy face, recur –
More dear art thou, O fair and fragile blossom;
Dearest when most thy tender traits express
The image of thy mother's loveliness.

PERCY BYSSHE SHELLEY

Mater Triumphans

Son of my woman's body, you go, to the drums and fife,
To taste the colour of love and the other side of life –
From out of the dainty the rude, the strong from out of
the frail,
Eternally through the ages from the female comes the
male.

The ten fingers and toes, and the shell-like nail on each.
The eyes blind as gems and the tongue attempting speech;
Impotent hands in my bosom, and yet they shall wield the
sword!
Drugged with slumber and milk, you wait the day of the
Lord.

Infant bridegroom, uncrowned king, unanointed priest,
Soldier, lover, explorer, I see you nuzzle the breast.
You that grope in my bosom shall load the ladies with
rings,
You, that came forth through the doors shall burst the
doors of kings.

R. L. Stevenson

from Wishes to My Son, John

For this new, and all succeeding years:
January 1, 1630

If wishes may enrich my boy,
My Jack, that art thy father's joy,
They shall be showered upon thy head
As thick as manna, angels' bread:
And bread I wish thee – this short word
Will furnish both thy back and board.

May a pure soul inhabit still
This well mixed clay, and a straight will
Biased by reason, that by grace.
May gems of price maintain their place
In such a casket: in that list
Chaste turquoise, sober amethyst.

Peace I do wish thee from those wars
Which gownmen talk out at the bars
Four times a year: I wish thee peace
Of conscience, country, and increase
In all that best of men commends,
Favour with God, good men thy friends.

Last, for lasting legacy
I this bequeath, when thou shalt die,
Heaven's monarch bless mine eyes, to see
My wishes crowned, in crowning thee.

HENRY KING

To Iva, Two and a Half

Little fat baby, as we
don't run the world, I
wince that I can't
drive a car or truck, ice-
skate, build shelves and
tables, ride
you up five flights of
stairs on my shoulders.
I notice you noticing
who rides most of the Big
Motorcyles, drives buses,
stacks grocery cartons, makes
loud big holes in the street.
'Mustn't hit little girls!' meaning
you, though who'd
know if we didn't say so!
Soon they'll be tellling you
you can't be
Batman, Shakespeare, President or God.
Little fat baby, going on
schoolgirl, you can be
anyone, but it won't be
easy.

MARILYN HACKER

Fain Would I Dive

Fain would I dive to find my infant self
In the unfathom'd ocean of the past:
I can but find a sun-burnt prattling elf,
A forward urchin of four years at least.

The prettiest speech – 'tis in my mind engrain'd-
That first awaked me from my babyhood,
Twas a grave saw affectionately feign'd-
'We'll love you little master, – if you're good.'

Sweet babe thou art not yet or good or bad,
Yet God is round thee, in thee, and above thee;
We love, because we love thee, little lad,
And pray thou may'st be good – because we love thee.

HARTLEY COLERIDGE

De Profundis

Out of the deep, my child, out of the deep,
Where all that was to be, in all that was,
Whirl'd for a million aeons thro' the vast
Waste dawn of multitudinous-eddying light –
Out of the deep, my child, out of the deep,
Thro' all this changing world of changeless law,
And every phase of ever-heightening life,
And nine long months of antenatal gloom,
With this last moon, this crescent – her dark orb
Touch'd with earth's light – thou comest, darling boy;
Our own; a babe in lineament and limb
Perfect, and prophet of the perfect man;
Whose face and form are hers and mine in one,
Indissolubly married like our love;
Live, and be happy in thyself, and serve
This mortal race thy kin so well, that men
May bless thee as we bless thee, O young life
Breaking with laughter from the dark; and may
The fated channel where thy motion lives
Be prosperously shaped, and sway thy course
Along the years of haste and random youth
Unshatter'd; then full-current thro' full man;
And last in kindly curves, with gentlest fall,
By quiet fields, a slowly-dying power,
To that last deep where we and thou are still.

ALFRED, LORD TENNYSON

Heavy As Lead

I

For our children are the children of our flesh
And the body of our love. The love that was
Before child-birth seems airy, feathery,
Frond-like now, a spirit moving grass.

Lovers' love which is a spirit must take
Flesh, the bodies we beget and bear;
And flesh is heavy and opaque
And a lodestone to care.

II

Heavy as lead, heavy as water
That seeks with obdurate art
And finds for resting-place the deepest part,
So heavy in us is our tender daughter.

Heavy in us – to God or stranger
A spirit or leaf-light sapling,
To us she is a leaden anchor grappling
To sand and central rock: the ocean-ranger

Strains against it. Heavy as earth
On a tree's roots when the green tree,

Its sunward frame, is racing like a sea.
So heavy is child-love, and holds us as if she,
Our child, were ground that gave us birth.

E. J. SCOVELL

from Nothing Is Lost

Nothing dies.
The cells pass on their secrets, we betray them
Unknowingly: in a freckle, in the way
We walk, recall some ancestor,
And Adam in the colour of our eyes.

Yes, on the face of the new born,
Before the soul has taken full possession,
There pass, as over a screen, in succession
The images of other beings:
Face after face looks out, and then is gone.

Nothing is lost, for all in love survive.
I lay my cheek against his sleeping limbs
To feel if he is warm, and touch in him
Those children whom no shawl could warm,
No arms, no grief, no longing could revive.

Thus what we see, or know,
Is only a tiny portion, at the best,
Of the life in which we share; an iceberg's crest
Our sunlit present, our partial sense,
With deep supporting multitudes below.

ANNE RIDLER

The Thread
The First Years

The First Birthday

The Sun, sweet girl, hath run his year-long race
Through the vast nothing of the eternal sky –
Since the glad hearing of the first faint cry
Announc'd a stranger from the unknown place
Of unborn souls. How blank was then the face,
How uninform'd the weak light-shunning eye,
That wept and saw not. Poor mortality
Begins to mourn before it knows its case,
Prophetic in its ignorance. But soon
The hospitalities of earth engage
The banish'd spirit in its new exile –
Pass some few changes of the fickle Moon,
The merry babe has learn'd its mother's smile,
Its Father's frown, its Nurse's mimic rage.

HARTLEY COLERIDGE

The Thread

Jamie made his landing in the world
so hard he ploughed straight back into the earth.
They caught him by the thread of his one breath
and pulled him up. They don't know how it held.
And so today I thank what higher will
brought us to here, to you and me and Russ,
the great twin-engined swaying wingspan of us
roaring down the back of Kirrie Hill

and your two-year-old lungs somehow out-revving
every engine in the universe.
All that trouble just to turn up dead
was all I thought that long week. Now the thread
is holding all of us: look at our tiny house,
son, the white dot of your mother waving.

DON PATERSON

Mother and Daughter

XVI

She will not have it that my day wanes low,
Poor of the fire its drooping sun denies,
That on my brow the thin lines write goodbyes
Which soon may be read plain for all to know,
Tellling that I have done with youth's brave show;
Alas! and done with youth in hearts and eyes,
With wonder and with far expectancies,
Save but to say 'I knew such long ago.'

She will not have it. Loverlike to me,
She with her happy gaze finds all that's best,
She sees this fair and that unfretted still,
And her own sunshine over all the rest;
So she half keeps me as she'd have me be,
And I forget to age, through her sweet will.

AUGUSTA WEBSTER

Frost at Midnight

The frost performs its secret ministry,
Unhelped by any wind. The owlet's cry
Came loud – and hark, again! loud as before.
The inmates of my cottage, all at rest,
Have left me to that solitude, which suits
Abstruser musings: save that at my side
My cradled infant slumbers peacefully.
'Tis calm indeed! so calm, that it disturbs
And vexes meditation with its strange
And extreme silentness. Sea, hill, and wood,
This populous village! Sea, and hill, and wood,
With all the numberless goings on of life,
Inaudible as dreams! the thin blue flame
Lies on my low burnt fire, and quivers not;
Only that film, which fluttered on the grate,
Still flutters there, the sole unquiet thing.
Methinks, its motion in this hush of nature
Gives it dim sympathies with me who live,
Making it a companionable form,
Whose puny flaps and freaks the idling Spirit
By its own moods interprets, every where
Echo or mirror seeking of itself,
And makes a toy of Thought.

But O! how oft,
How oft, at school, with most believing mind,
Presageful, have I gazed upon the bars,
To watch that fluttering stranger! and as oft

With unclosed lids, already had I dreamt
Of my sweet birth-place, and the old church-tower,
Whose bells, the poor man's only music, rang
From morn to evening, all the hot Fair-day,
So sweetly, that they stirred and haunted me
With a wild pleasure, falling on mine ear
Most like articulate sounds of things to come!
So gazed I, till the soothing things I dreamt
Lulled me to sleep, and sleep prolonged my dreams!
And so I brooded all the following morn,
Awed by the stern preceptor's face, mine eye
Fixed with mock study on my swimming book:
Save if the door half opened, and I snatched
A hasty glance, and still my heart leaped up,
For still I hoped to see the stranger's face,
Townsman, or aunt, or sister more beloved,
My play-mate when we both were clothed alike!

Dear Babe, that sleepest cradled by my side,
Whose gentle breathings, heard in this deep calm,
Fill up the interspersed vacancies
And momentary pauses of the thought!
My babe so beautiful! it thrills my heart
With tender gladness, thus to look at thee,
And think that thou shalt learn far other lore
And in far other scenes! For I was reared
In the great city, pent 'mid cloisters dim,
And saw nought lovely but the sky and stars.
But thou, my babe! shalt wander like a breeze
By lakes and sandy shores, beneath the crags
Of ancient mountain, and beneath the clouds,
Which image in their bulk both lakes and shores

And mountain crags: so shalt thou see and hear
The lovely shapes and sounds intelligible
Of that eternal language, which thy God
Utters, who from eternity doth teach
Himself in all, and all things in himself.
Great universal Teacher! he shall mould
Thy spirit, and by giving make it ask.

Therefore all seasons shall be sweet to thee,
Whether the summer clothe the general earth
With greenness, or the redbreast sit and sing
Betwixt the tufts of snow on the bare branch
Of mossy apple-tree, while the nigh thatch
Smokes in the sun-thaw; whether the eave-drops fall
Heard only in the trances of the blast,
Or if the secret ministry of frost
Shall hang them up in silent icicles,
Quietly shining to the quiet Moon.

SAMUEL TAYLOR COLERIDGE

Two Breaths

Alfie on Christmas Eve. Her breath is caught,
let out in shots,
unsettled and unique with thinking things
we said will happen.

My breath, expecting nothing, is so calm
it measures time,
or passes for it, so if time could hear
it would hear silence.

GLYN MAXWELL

Haunts

Don't be afraid, old son, it's only me,
though not as I've appeared before,
on the battlements of your signature,
or margin of a book you can't throw out,
or darkened shop front where your face
first shocks itself into a mask of mine,
but here, alive, one Christmas long ago
when you were three, upstairs, asleep,
and haunting me because I conjured you
the way that child you were would cry out
waking in the dark, and when you spoke
in no child's voice but out of radio silence,
the hall clock ticking like a radar blip,
a bottle breaking faintly streets away,
you said, as I say now, *Don't be afraid*.

MICHAEL DONAGHY
27 December 1999

Ode on the Whole Duty of Parents

The spirits of children are remote and wise,
They must go free
Like fishes in the sea
Or starlings in the skies,
Whilst you remain
The shore where casually they come again.
But when there falls the stalking shade of fear,
You must be suddenly near,
You, the unstable, must become a tree
In whose unending heights of flowering green
Hangs every fruit that grows, with silver bells;
Where heart-distracting magic birds are seen
And all the things a fairy-story tells;
Though still you should possess
Roots that go deep in ordinary earth,
And strong consoling bark
To love and to caress.

Last, when at dark
Safe on the pillow lies an up-gazing head
And drinking holy eyes
Are fixed on you,
When, from behind them, questions come to birth
Insistently,
On all the things that you have ever said
Of suns and snakes and parallelograms and flies,
Then for a while you'll need to be no more
That sheltering shore

Or legendary tree in safety spread,
No, then you must put on
The robes of Solomon,
Or simply be
Sir Isaac Newton sitting on the bed.

FRANCES CORNFORD

The Mother

In the dreamy silence after bath,
hot in the milk-white towel, my son
announces that I will not love him when I'm dead
because people can't think when they're dead. I can't
think at first – not love him? The air outside the
window is very black, the old locust
beginning to lose its leaves already . . .
I hold him tight, he is white as a buoy
and my death like dark water is rising
swiftly in the room. I tell him I loved him
before he was born. I do not tell him
I'm damned if I won't love him after I'm
dead, necessity after all being
the mother of invention.

SHARON OLDS

Demeter

Where I lived – winter and hard earth.
I sat in my cold stone room
choosing tough words, granite, flint,

to break the ice. My broken heart –
I tried that, but it skimmed,
flat, over the frozen lake.

She came from a long, long way,
but I saw her at last, walking,
my daughter, my girl, across the fields,

in bare feet, bringing all spring's flowers
to her mother's house. I swear
the air softened and warmed as she moved,

the blue sky smiling, none too soon,
with the small shy mouth of a new moon.

CAROL ANN DUFFY

On Children

How dull our days, how lacking in surprise
Without these small epitomes of sin,
These flowers with their store of life within
And grave, appalling freshness in their eyes.

FRANCES CORNFORD

Index of Authors and Translators

Index of Titles and First Lines